What time is it?

Bobbie Kalman

Crabtree Publishing Company

www.crabtreebooks.com

Created by Bobbie Kalman

Dedicated by Ken Wright,
For Oliver and Simon Regier, "The only reason for time is so that everything doesn't happen at once."

Author and Editor-in-Chief
Bobbie Kalman

Editor
Kathy Middleton

Proofreader
Crystal Sikkens

Photo research
Bobbie Kalman
Crystal Sikkens

Design
Bobbie Kalman
Katherine Berti
Samantha Crabtree (logo and front cover)

Production coordinator
Katherine Berti

Illustrations
Barbara Bedell: page 10 (flower)
Bonna Rouse: page 5
Margaret Amy Salter: page 10 (butterflies)

Photographs
© iStockphoto.com: page 13 (top left)
© Shutterstock.com: All other images

Library and Archives Canada Cataloguing in Publication

Kalman, Bobbie, 1947-
    What time is it? / Bobbie Kalman.

(Looking at nature)
Includes index.
ISBN 978-0-7787-3325-6 (bound).--ISBN 978-0-7787-3345-4 (pbk.)

    1. Time--Juvenile literature. 2. Seasons--Juvenile literature.
I. Title. II. Series: Kalman, Bobbie, 1947- . Looking at nature.

QB209.5.K35 2008   j529   C2008-907021-6

Library of Congress Cataloging-in-Publication Data

Kalman, Bobbie.
    What time is it? / Bobbie Kalman.
        p. cm. -- (Looking at nature)
    Includes index.
    ISBN 978-0-7787-3345-4 (pbk. : alk. paper) -- ISBN 978-0-7787-3325-6
(reinforced lib. bdg. : alk. paper)
    1. Time--Juvenile literature. 2. Seasons--Juvenile literature. I. Title.
II. Series.

QB209.5.K35 2009
529--dc22
                                                    2008046271

Crabtree Publishing Company

www.crabtreebooks.com   1-800-387-7650

Published in Canada
Crabtree Publishing
616 Welland Ave.
St. Catharines, Ontario
L2M 5V6

Published in the United States
Crabtree Publishing
PMB16A
350 Fifth Ave., Suite 3308
New York, NY 10118

Published in the United Kingdom
Crabtree Publishing
White Cross Mills
High Town, Lancaster
LA1 4XS

Published in Australia
Crabtree Publishing
386 Mt. Alexander Rd.
Ascot Vale (Melbourne)
VIC 3032

Contents

What time is it?

We wake up in the morning. The sun is in the sky. What time is it? It is daytime, and it is today. When we went to bed last night, it was yesterday. We will go to bed again tonight. When we wake up the next day, it will be tomorrow. Make a list of all the words on this page that talk about time.

We have breakfast in the morning.

We go to bed at nighttime.

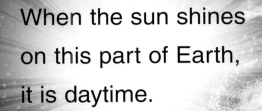

When the sun shines
on this part of Earth,
it is daytime.

This part of Earth is
not getting sunlight.
It is nighttime here.

Time words:
morning, daytime,
nighttime, today, tonight,
yesterday, tomorrow,
last night, next day

How do we tell time?

What time is it? How do we tell time? We use clocks or **watches** to tell time. Some clocks are round like this one. They have hands that tell you what hour, minute, and second it is. What time does this clock say it is?

We wear watches to tell the time.

minute hand

second hand

hour hand

The time is 5:01 and 11 seconds!

6

Some clocks and watches are **digital**. Digital clocks use **digits**, or numbers, to show the time.

digital clock

What kind of clock wakes us up? An ***alarm clock*** *does!*

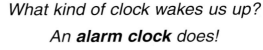

This child is using a small computer called a ***Personal Digital Assistant*** *(PDA) to tell time.*

What time is this boy showing? His hands show ten minutes to four o'clock!

7

A year of time

What day, week, or month is it? Calendars show us weeks, months, or a whole year at once. How many days are in a week? Which month has 28 days? Which months have 30 days? Which ones have 31 days? How many days are in a year? Did you know that there are 365 days in a year?

January

S	M	T	W	T	F	S
				1	2	3
4	5	6	7	8	9	10
11	12	13	14	15	16	17
18	19	20	21	22	23	24
25	26	27	28	29	30	31

February

S	M	T	W	T	F	S
1	2	3	4	5	6	7
8	9	10	11	12	13	14
15	16	17	18	19	20	21
22	23	24	25	26	27	28

March

S	M	T	W	T	F	S
1	2	3	4	5	6	7
8	9	10	11	12	13	14
15	16	17	18	19	20	21
22	23	24	25	26	27	28
29	30	31				

April

S	M	T	W	T	F	S
			1	2	3	4
5	6	7	8	9	10	11
12	13	14	15	16	17	18
19	20	21	22	23	24	25
26	27	28	29	30		

May

S	M	T	W	T	F	S
					1	2
3	4	5	6	7	8	9
10	11	12	13	14	15	16
17	18	19	20	21	22	23
24	25	26	27	28	29	30
31						

June

S	M	T	W	T	F	S
	1	2	3	4	5	6
7	8	9	10	11	12	13
14	15	16	17	18	19	20
21	22	23	24	25	26	27
28	29	30				

July

S	M	T	W	T	F	S
			1	2	3	4
5	6	7	8	9	10	11
12	13	14	15	16	17	18
19	20	21	22	23	24	25
26	27	28	29	30	31	

August

S	M	T	W	T	F	S
						1
2	3	4	5	6	7	8
9	10	11	12	13	14	15
16	17	18	19	20	21	22
23	24	25	26	27	28	29
30	31					

September

S	M	T	W	T	F	S
		1	2	3	4	5
6	7	8	9	10	11	12
13	14	15	16	17	18	19
20	21	22	23	24	25	26
27	28	29	30			

October

S	M	T	W	T	F	S
				1	2	3
4	5	6	7	8	9	10
11	12	13	14	15	16	17
18	19	20	21	22	23	24
25	26	27	28	29	30	31

November

S	M	T	W	T	F	S
1	2	3	4	5	6	7
8	9	10	11	12	13	14
15	16	17	18	19	20	21
22	23	24	25	26	27	28
29	30					

December

S	M	T	W	T	F	S
		1	2	3	4	5
6	7	8	9	10	11	12
13	14	15	16	17	18	19
20	21	22	23	24	25	26
27	28	29	30	31		

On a calendar, we can mark down special days such as birthdays. Which special days do you want to remember? Do you mark down the dates of your sports games?

*Do you write in a **journal** every day? What do you write about?*

Don't forget Mother's Day!

Do you know the birthdays of your best friends? What gifts will you give them?

What are seasons?

We can also tell time by **seasons**. In many parts of the world, there are four seasons. They are spring, summer, autumn or fall, and winter. A season lasts about three months. It has certain **weather**. Weather is the amount of sunshine, rain or snow, wind, and heat in an area.

In which season do flowers start to bloom?

12

The days start getting more sunlight, and the weather gets warmer. Plants start growing new leaves and flowers. Do you know which season it is? Plants and animals know that it is springtime!

frog eggs

Frogs wake up from their winter sleep and lay eggs.

Many baby animals are born in springtime. These baby lambs were just born. Their mother is cleaning them.

It's summertime!

Fruits and vegetables grow bigger in the summertime. Some vegetables and fruits are **ripe**, or ready to eat. Other fruits **ripen**, or become ripe, at the end of summer. Apples and pears ripen near the end of summer.

Baby animals that were born in the spring have grown by summer. Their mothers show them where to find food to eat.

*These moose **calves**, or young moose, are learning which plants are good to eat.*

This bear cub is crying. He needs his mother!

These baby pigs and their mother are looking for food in a field. Follow the leader!

Autumn or fall?

Which season comes after summer? Autumn does! The days start getting less sunlight. When there is less sunlight, it gets colder. Leaves change color, and they soon fall off the trees. Is that why "fall" is another name for this season? What do you call this season?

Do animals know what time it is? Fall is the time for some animals to go into a deep sleep. This sleep is called **hibernation**. Some animals **migrate** to places that have warm winters. To migrate is to move to another place. The amount of sunlight tells animals when to hibernate or migrate.

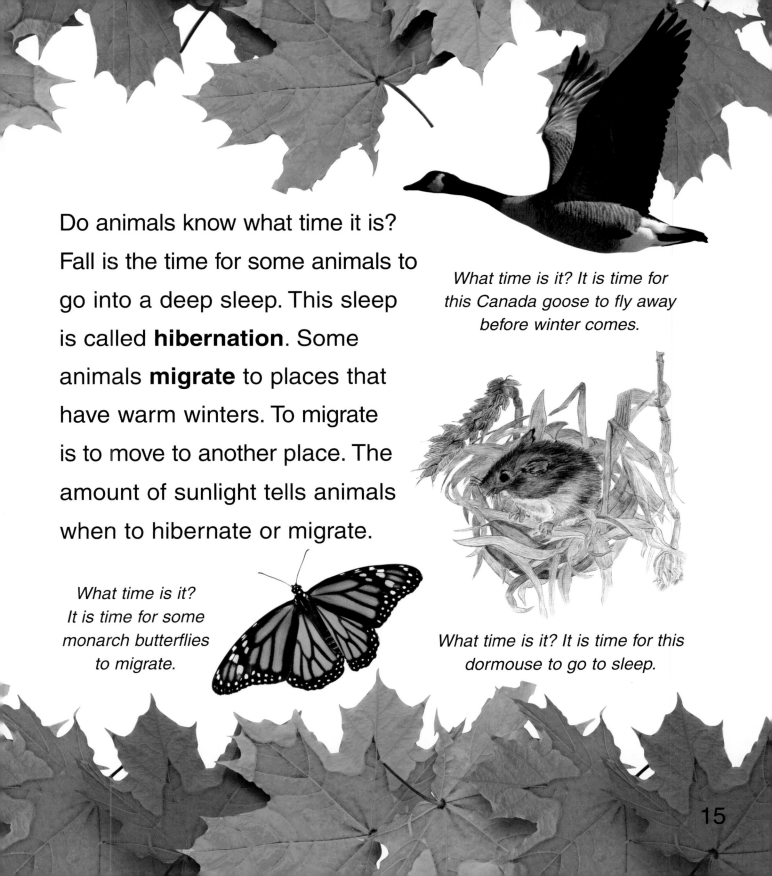

What time is it? It is time for this Canada goose to fly away before winter comes.

What time is it? It is time for some monarch butterflies to migrate.

What time is it? It is time for this dormouse to go to sleep.

15

It's wintertime!

When does nature sleep? It sleeps in the wintertime! Winter days have much less sunlight. In many places, the ground is covered with snow and ice. Winter is the coldest time of the year. Plants and many animals are asleep. Other animals have a hard time finding food.

These wild horses have found grass to eat under the snow.

This squirrel has found a nut in the snow.

This cardinal is looking for some seeds to eat.

This red fox has grown a warm fur coat and a thick tail for the winter.

Your favorite season

Which is your favorite season? Is it spring, summer, winter, or fall? Write a story or poem about your favorite time of the year or paint a picture of your favorite season.

Write a story about your favorite Halloween or Christmas.

Share the story of your very best summer!

How big was the biggest snowman you ever made?

Paint a picture of springtime flowers.

When was long ago?

What time was **long ago**? Was it ten years, hundreds of years, thousands of years, or millions of years ago? These pictures show times in **history**. History is what happened in the **past**. It is the stories of long ago. Guess how long ago it was in each of these pictures!

Did dinosaurs live tens, hundreds, thousands, or millions of years ago?

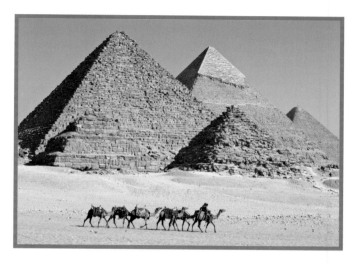

*How old are these **pyramids** in Egypt?*
Pyramids are buildings that have sides
with triangle shapes.

Was this boy
born a thousand
years ago?

*When did soldiers called **knights** ride horses? Was it ten years ago?*

Answers:

Dinosaurs lived millions of years ago.

The pyramids are thousands of years old.

Knights lived hundreds of years ago.

The boy was born about ten years ago.

The present is a gift

The past is what happened last week, last month, last year, and many years before that. The past can also be a few minutes ago, but now it is gone. The **future** has not yet happened. It is something that will happen tomorrow, next week, next year, and many years from now. Only the **present** is here now. It is a gift. Is that why we call it the present? What are you doing with your present?

What can you do right now? You can be a good friend. You can be kind to everyone you meet.

What time is it? It is the wonderful present. The present is the only time to be happy. Wear a big smile, and your joy will spread to others. This is a beautiful moment, and now is the perfect time!

Words to know and Index

autumn/fall
pages 10, 14, 15, 18

calendars
pages 8–9

clocks
pages 6–7

hibernation
page 15

long ago
pages 20–21

migration
page 15

spring
pages 10, 11, 13, 18, 19

Other index words
day pages 4, 5, 8, 9, 11, 14, 16
future page 22
history page 20
month pages 8, 10, 22
past pages 20, 22
present pages 22–23
seasons pages 10–19
today pages 4, 5
tomorrow pages 4, 5, 22
weather pages 10, 11
week pages 8, 22
year pages 8, 20, 21, 22
yesterday pages 4, 5

summer
pages 10, 12, 13, 14, 18, 19

watches
pages 6–7

winter
pages 10, 11, 15, 16, 17, 18

DISCARDED